Creation's First Light

Written by Sandy Eisenberg Sasso
Illustrated by Joani Rothenberg

To Darwin, Ari and Levi
For the light of your souls
and the joy you bring.

SES

Nonie and David
Your friendship means the world to me.

JKR

Text by Sandy Eisenberg Sasso
Illustrations by Joani Keller Rothenberg
Book Design by Alexandra Springman Segal and Sarah Philippart

ISBN: 978-1-934922-94-1
First Edition

Library of Congress Control Number: 2013943384

Copyright 2013 by IBJ Book Publishing.

ALL RIGHTS RESERVED. No part of this book may be reproduced in any manner without the express written consent of the publisher.

June 2013, Printed by Everbest Printing (Guangzhou, China), Co. Ltd. - 113043

Published & distributed by:
IBJ Book Publishing, 41 E. Washington St., Suite 200, Indianapolis, IN 46204, www.ibjbp.com

On the first day of creation, God said, "Let there be light," and there was light and nothing else.

God made the sky on the second day.

On day number three, God made the seas
and the land, the plants and the trees.

But the light of the sun and the moon was different than the light of the first day.

With the first day's light you could create a whole world.

That first light made possible all the other days of creation.

But when Adam and Eve did not listen to God and ate from the Tree of Knowledge of Good and Evil, God hid that light.

Some say it is hidden in the words of the ancient ones.

And with that light, God created stories.

Some say that Adam and Eve carried a small ray of that light in a jewel.

It shone there for forty days and nights.

From that light, God made a rainbow.

Then the light disappeared, until Abraham found it glowing in a cave.

Abraham gave it to Isaac and Isaac to Jacob.

Jacob passed it on to Joseph.

By that light,

Joseph dreamed.

Moses found it and placed it above the tablets of the Ten Commandments.

By that light, Miriam danced.

**Some say that after Moses and Miriam,
Creation's first light was lost forever.**

There was only the light of the sun, the moon and the stars.

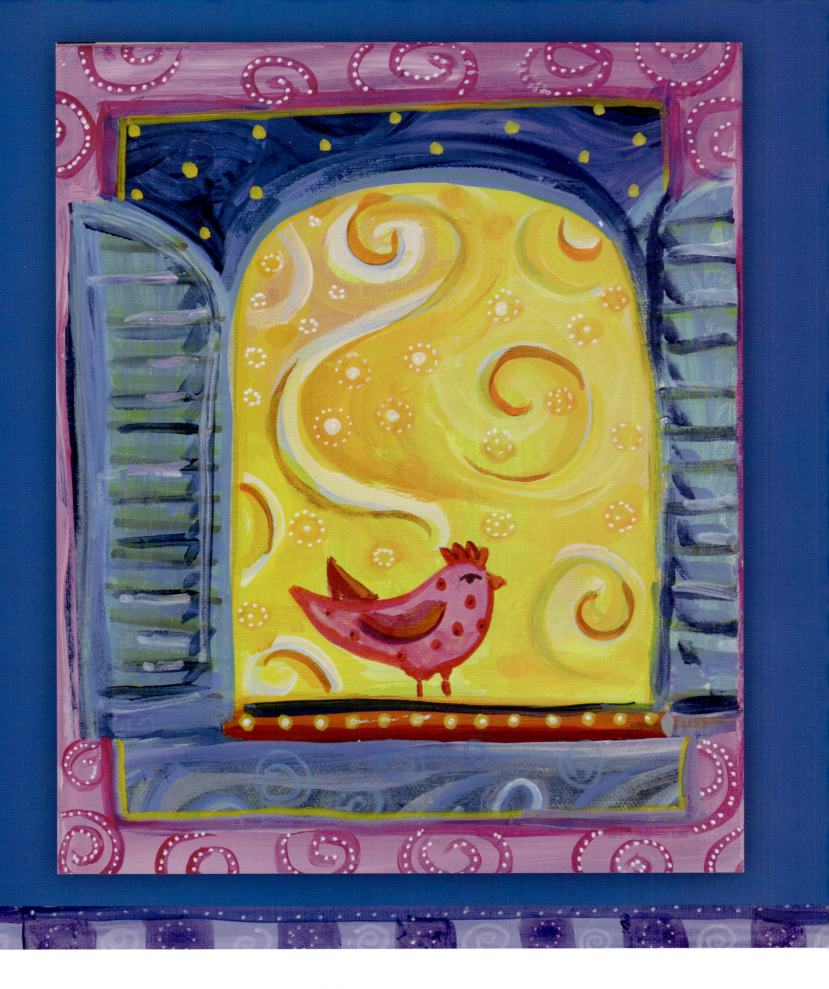

But I will let you in on a secret.

There are places where you can find that light.

It peeks out from behind a giant smile.

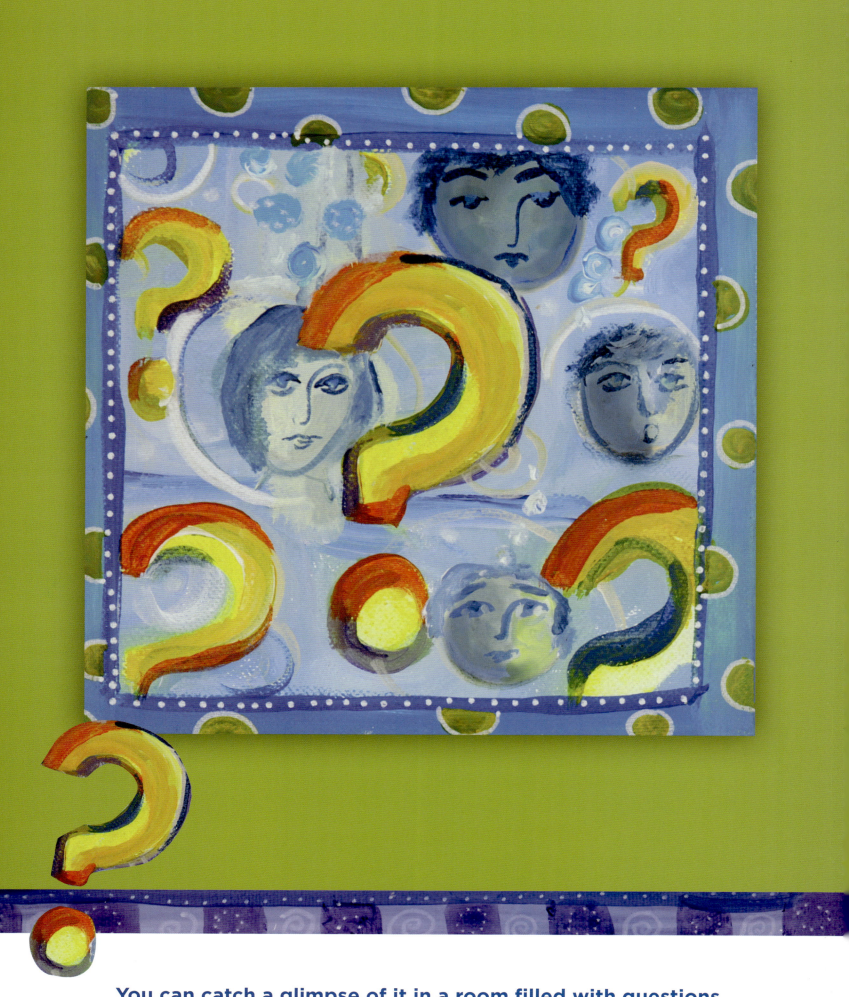

You can catch a glimpse of it in a room filled with questions.

It winks at you in a meadow full of memories.

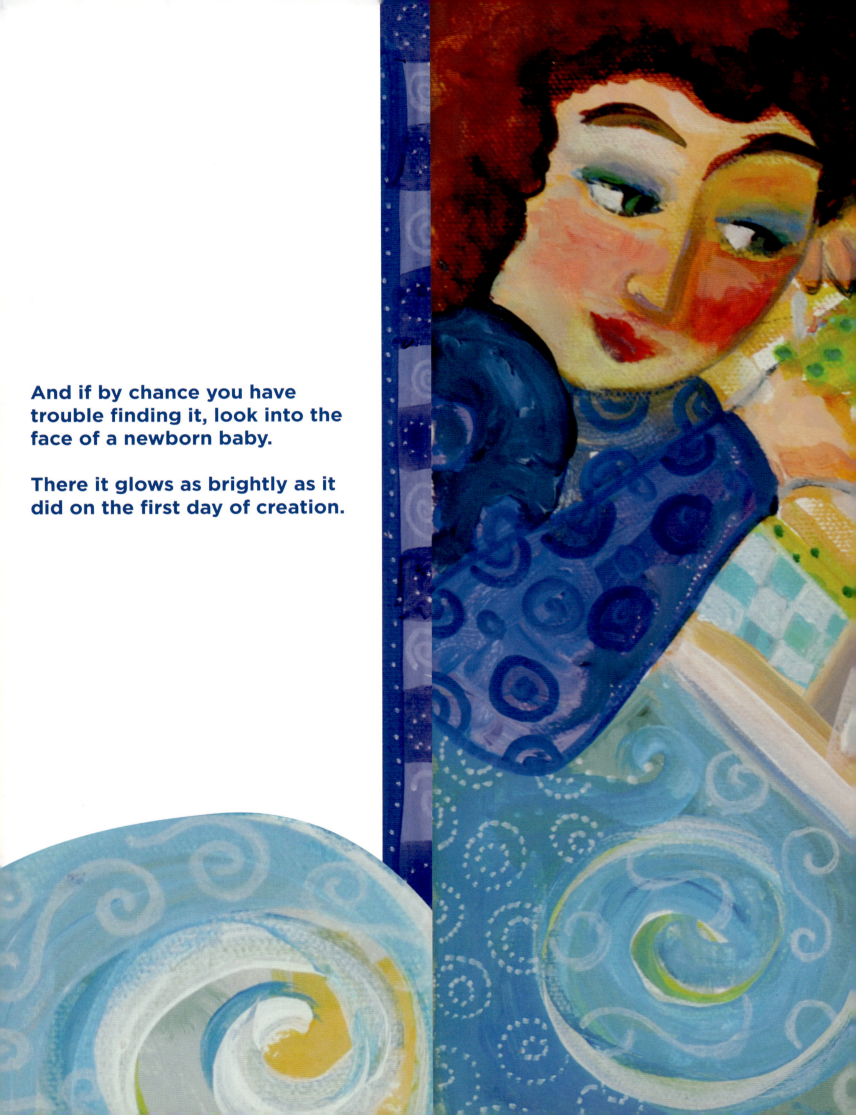

And if by chance you have trouble finding it, look into the face of a newborn baby.

There it glows as brightly as it did on the first day of creation.

Your great grandparents carried that light within them.
They passed it on to your grandparents.

Your grandparents gave it to your parents.

Then your parents took that light and passed it on to you while you were still waiting to be born.

If you look deep inside yourself, you will find that light.

The light has a name.

For Parents and Teachers:

***

Adam and Eve made a choice to eat from the Tree of Knowledge of Good and Evil in the Garden of Eden, even though God told them not to eat from that tree.

Do you ever make wrong choices?
What good choices have you made?

(You will find the story of Adam and Eve in Genesis 2-3.)

***

Noah built an ark and saved the world from destruction. The story teaches us that people can destroy the world but they can also save it.

What are some things that you do that mess up the world?
What can you do to fix up the world?

(You will find the story of Noah in Genesis 6-9.)

***

The Bible tells us that God told Abraham, "Go forth from your native land and from your parents' house to the land that I will show you." It took courage to leave a well-known place and go to an unfamiliar place.

What gives you the courage to do something you have never done before?

(You will find the story of Abraham in Genesis 12-25.)

***

***

Joseph was one of 12 brothers and one sister.
When he was young, he dreamed of becoming a leader.
He never forgot his dream and eventually he became
prime minister of Egypt.

What do you dream?

(You will find the story of Joseph in Genesis 37, 39–50. Joseph's dreams
and his interpretation of Pharaoh's dreams are in Genesis 37, 40-41.)

***

Moses gave the people of Israel rules to guide them.
Those rules are called the Ten Commandments or the Ten Words.

What do you think are the most important words?

(You will find the Ten Commandments in Exodus 20 and Deuteronomy 5.)

***

Miriam helped lead the people of Israel across a sea to freedom.
The first thing she did when she crossed the sea was to dance.

What makes you so happy that you want to dance?

(You will find the story of the crossing of the sea in Exodus 13–15.)

***